Ulrich Renz / Barbara Brin

Sleep Tight, Little Wolf

Dors bien, petit loup

A picture book in two languages

Translation:

Pete Savill, Lübeck, Germany (English)

Céleste Lottigier, Toulouse, France (French)

Little Wolf would like to meet you at his home:

www.childrens-books-bilingual.com

"Good night, Tim! We'll continue searching tomorrow.
Now sleep tight!"

"Bonne nuit, Tim! On continuera à chercher demain.
Dors bien maintenant!"

It is already dark outside.

Dehors, il fait déjà nuit.

What is Tim doing?

Mais que fait Tim là?

He is leaving for the playground.

What is he looking for there?

Il va dehors, à l'aire de jeu.

Qu'est-ce qu'il y cherche?

The little wolf!

He can't sleep without it.

Le petit loup!

Sans lui, il ne peut pas dormir.

Who's this coming?

Mais qui arrive là?

Marie!

She's looking for her ball.

Marie!

Elle cherche son ballon.

And what is Tobi looking for?

Et Tobi, qu'est-ce qu'il cherche?

His digger.

Sa pelleteuse.

And what is Nala looking for?

Et Nala, qu'est-ce qu'elle cherche?

Her doll.

Sa poupée.

Don't the children have to go to bed?

The cat is rather surprised.

Les enfants ne doivent-ils pas aller au lit ?

Le chat est très surpris.

Who's coming now?

Qui vient donc là?

Tim's mum and dad!

They can't sleep without their Tim.

Le papa et la maman de Tim!

Sans leur Tim, ils ne peuvent pas dormir.

More of them are coming! Marie's dad.
Tobi's grandpa. And Nala's mum.

Et en voilà encore d'autres qui arrivent!
Le papa de Marie. Le papi de Tobi. Et la maman de Nala.

Now hurry to bed everyone!

Vite au lit maintenant!

"Good night, Tim!
Tomorrow we won't have to search any longer."

"Bonne nuit, Tim!
Demain nous n'aurons plus besoin de chercher."

"Sleep tight, little wolf!"

"Dors bien, petit loup!"

More about me ...

Que duermas bien, pequeño lobo
Schlaf gut, kleiner Wolf

Ulrich Renz / Barbara Brinkmann

español | bilingüe | alemán

Schlaf gut, kleiner Wolf
راحت بخواب، گرگ کوچک

Ulrich Renz / Barbara Brinkmann

Deutsch | bilingual | Persisch (Farsi)

Dors bien, petit loup
Sleep Tight, Little Wolf

Ulrich Renz / Barbara Brinkmann

français | bilingue | anglais

نم جيدا أيها الذئب الصغير
Sov gott, lilla vargen

Ulrich Renz / Barbara Brinkmann

العربية | ثنائي اللغة | السويدية

Sofðu rótt, litli úlfur
Όνειρα γλυκά, μικρέ λύκε

Ulrich Renz / Barbara Brinkmann

Íslenska | tvímála | gríska

Dorme bem, lobinho
Suaviter dormi, lupe parve

Ulrich Renz / Barbara Brinkmann

português | bilingue | latino

Schlaf gut, kleiner Wolf
おおかみくんも
ぐっすり　おやすみなさい

Ulrich Renz / Barbara Brinkmann

Deutsch | bilingual | Japanisch

잘 자, 꼬마 늑대야
Slaap lekker, kleine wolf

Ulrich Renz / Barbara Brinkmann

한국어 | 양국어 | 네덜란드어

Приятных снов, маленький волчёнок
Sleep Tight, Little Wolf

Ulrich Renz / Barbara Brinkmann

русский | двуязычный | английский

راحت بخواب، گرگ کوچک
Schlaf gut, kleiner Wolf

Ulrich Renz / Barbara Brinkmann

فارسی | دوزبانی | آلمانی

Que duermas bien, pequeño lobo
نم جيداً أيها الذئب الصغير

Ulrich Renz / Barbara Brinkmann

español | bilingüe | árabe

സുഖമായി ഉറങ്ങൂ
ചെന്നായി കുഞ്ഞേ
Dormi bene, piccolo lupo

Ulrich Renz / Barbara Brinkmann

മലയാളം | ദ്വിഭാഷാ | ഇറ്റാലിയൻ

Dormi bene, piccolo lupo
जम के सोना , छोटे भेड़िये

Ulrich Renz / Barbara Brinkmann

italiano | bilinguale | hindi

�አ ድቃስ፡ ንእሽቶይ ተኹላ
Selamat tidur, si serigala

Ulrich Renz / Barbara Brinkmann

ትግርኛ | ብ ኽልተ ቋንቋ | Malaysian

Śpij dobrze, mały wilku
ძილო ნებისა, პატარა მგელო

Ulrich Renz / Barbara Brinkmann

polski | Dwujęzyczna | gruziński

Солодких снів, маленький вовчику
잘 자, 꼬마 늑대야

Ulrich Renz / Barbara Brinkmann

українська | двомовний | корейська

A Children's Book
for the Global Village

"Sleep Tight, Little Wolf" is a multilingual picture book for the ever growing number of children who face the challenge – and the opportunity – of living with different cultures and languages. Their families may have been displaced to another country as refugees. Or their parents may have chosen the life of expats, working for a global company or an NGO. Perhaps it may merely have been love that brought together two people from different world regions who don't even speak the same language.

Migration and ensuing multilingualism is a global megatrend of our days. Ever more children are born away from their parents' home countries, and are balancing between the languages of their mother, their father, their grandparents, and their peers. "Sleep Tight, Little Wolf" is meant to help bridge the language divides that cross more and more families, neighborhoods and kindergartens in the globalized world. This is a global picture book – coming to you in more than 50 languages and all conceivable bilingual combinations of them.

www.childrens-books-bilingual.com

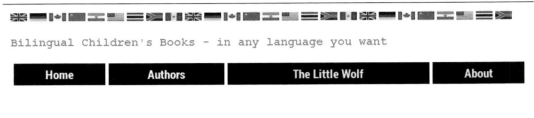

Bilingual Children's Books - in any language you want

Home	Authors	The Little Wolf	About

Welcome to the **Little Wolf's Language Wizard!**

Tell me, first of all, in which language you want me to work for you. English or German?

English ▾ Go!

Now just choose the two languages in which you want to read to your children:

Language 1:

Please choose... ▾

Language 2:

no 2nd language ▾

Go!

Learn more about the Little Wolf project at *www.childrens-books-bilingual.com.* At the heart of this website you will find what we call the "Little Wolf's Language Wizard". It contains more than 50 languages and any of their bilingual combinations: Just select, in a simple drop-down-menu, the two languages in which you'd like to read the story to your child – and the book is instantly made available, ready for order as an ebook download or as a printed edition.

As time goes by ...

... the little ones grow older, and start to read on their own. Here is Little Wolf's recommendation to them:

BO & FRIENDS

Smart detective stories for smart children

Reading age: 10 + - www.bo-and-friends.com

Wie die Zeit vergeht ...

Irgendwann sind aus den süßen Kleinen süße Große geworden

– die jetzt sogar selber lesen können. Der kleine Wolf empfiehlt:

MOTTE & CO

Kinderkrimis zum Mitdenken

Lesealter ab 10 – www.motte-und-co.de

About the authors

Ulrich Renz was born in Stuttgart, Germany, in 1960. After studying French literature in Paris he graduated from medical school in Lübeck and worked as head of a scientific publishing company. He is now a writer of non-fiction books as well as children's fiction books. – www.ulrichrenz.de

Barbara Brinkmann was born in Munich, Germany, in 1969. She grew up in the foothills of the Alps and studied architecture and medicine for a while in Munich. She now works as a freelance graphic artist, illustrator and writer. – www.bcbrinkmann.com

© 2016 by Sefa Verlag Kirsten Bödeker, Lübeck, Germany
www.sefa-verlag.de

ℬ sefa

Database: Paul Bödeker, Hamburg, Germany
Font: Noto Sans

ISBN: 9783739901459

Version: 20160225